THE FIVE-MINUTE GUIDE TO CREATING INVINCIBLE DEPONENTS

THE FIVE-MINUTE GUIDE TO CREATING INVINCIBLE DEPONENTS

JIM GARRITY, ESQ.

Ross and Rubin Publishers, LLC

New York, New York

Five-Minute Guide to Creating Invincible Deponents

Copyright © 2020 by Jim Garrity

EPIGRAPH

As Jim Garrity is famous for saying, "Depositions are the new trial." That's because virtually no civil case goes to trial. So the only place witnesses testify is in depositions. And that is where your case will be won or lost.

As with troops in battle, we must be thoroughly versed in conducting and defending depositions <u>before</u> our skills are called upon to achieve success. Yet because of the relative infrequency of actual deposition experiences in most trial lawyers' careers, we must seek to expand our understanding through other, less direct means.

The learned study of litigation tactics and techniques from the direct insights of ultra-high-volume litigators like Jim Garrity - who have deep, long-term experience - is an essential piece of our preparations, and of our development of judgment and insight. Guides like this enable us to see how successful trial lawyers have evaluated - and then handled - the situations they faced. Not many people can do it instinctively. Few possess a chessmaster's innate ability to visualize move and countermove dozens of steps ahead. Even those few can nonetheless build on their given talents through the study of the successes of others.

The experiences and shared expertise of others, then, provide the best source of indirect experience.

This book allows you to bulletproof your deponents. It tells you how to explain the deposition process, how to explain the role of opposing lawyers, and how to explain the way deposition transcripts are used. It offers genuinely brilliant insights on how to prep witnesses, and offers further tips on running them through a mock grinder examination.

If you follow Garrity's tips, you will see a striking increase in the strength of your cases, whether you represent plaintiffs or defendants.

— DAN JENNINGS

FOREWORD

Few of your cases will ever see the inside of a courtroom. They'll settle, or they'll be dismissed on procedural or substantive grounds.

So in civil cases, the bulk of your efforts must be devoted to discovery, and to depositions in particular. Some studies and anecdotal evidence show that many litigators spend thirty minutes or less preparing clients and witnesses for deposition. Often, that preparation takes place in the car on the way to the deposition, or even outside the offices of the court reporter or opposing lawyers. The preparation may be as shallow as telling deponents to remember what the case is about, to only answer the questions asked, and to limit answers to yes or no. Some lawyers make up for their lack of proper preparation by simply disrupting the deposition in progress, through obstructive objections and other tactics.

Poor preparation and disruptive conduct will not save your witnesses if the opposing lawyers have done their homework.

There is a way, though, to create invincible witnesses, and that is by making sure they thoroughly understand the role of the deposition, the role of the opposing lawyer, and the tricks and traps commonly used by trial lawyers to turn night into day, day into night, yes into no.

The chief problem in preparing deponents is that most witnesses perceive depositions as neutral events; that opposing lawyers ask simple, straightforward questions; and that lawyers accept whatever answer is given and move on. Some witnesses believe, perhaps based on TV and movies, they'll outfox the examiner with clever answers and non-answers.

Many witnesses trust opposing lawyers who say "I'm just here to find out what happened." Garrity says that if your deponents believe this, you've failed them. If your deponents start their depositions believing they can simply answer "yes" or "no," you've failed them. If your deponents aren't on high alert for misstatements of fact or law by the examining lawyer, and aren't on high alert for altered or fraudulent documents, you've failed them. And if your deponents don't fully appreciate how the transcript may be used, and the fact that they may never have a second chance to testify, you've failed them.

But if you've taken steps to bulletproof your deponents, you'll avoid these pitfalls, and the strength of your cases will grow sharply.

That's where this guide comes in. It contains decades of

in-the-trenches insights, tips and strategies about preparing deponents, all directly from Jim Garrity's own multistate litigation practice.

It's a thorough, methodical, systematic approach to creating invincible witnesses. It's not difficult, and it's not time-consuming. But you've got to use it. As you'll see, Garrity walks opponents through the deposition process, start to finish, always an eye-opener for those unfamiliar with the civil justice system. He ends deposition preparations with grinding, realistic mock examinations of the deponents, to get them accustomed to the tactics and tricks they'll encounter.

Deponents who have been through his preparation have described it as "fantastic," as a "stunning eye-opener." His deponents become rock solid, unshakable witnesses who swat aside even the most outrageous tactics from opposing lawyers.

This book, which is excerpted and revised from Jim Garrity's complete, 490-page practice masterwork on on the art and science of depositions, *10,000 Depositions Later: The Premier Litigation Guide for Superior Deposition Practice* (available on Amazon), is a timely, thoroughly-researched expert-level guide. It covers every conceivable issue and nuance in a short, enjoyable read. Make good use of it and good luck.

Stuart Barber

New York New York

PREFACE

Thank you for choosing this guide.

I decided to begin creating a series of advanced books and guides on deposition skills and techniques after reading studies showing that the civil trial in our judicial system is on the verge of complete extinction.

One legal scholar, Professor Marc Galanter, found that about only about one percent of all federal lawsuits now end in a trial. State court lawsuits have similarly fallen off the cliff. One article in a business publication, citing Professor Galanter's studies, was titled "Will There Be A Next Generation of Trial Lawyers?", underscoring the disappearance of the American court trial.

Without question, depositions are the new trials. That's because depositions are for most lawyers the only place any witness will ever testify. This means that in most lawsuits, the outcome is decided by deposition testimony.

There are many books for sale about deposition strategies and tactics. So, what hasn't been written already? The answer is, everything.

The books, treatises, and seminars for sale overwhelmingly address the mechanical aspects of depositions. They tell us to organize documents, to mark exhibits as we use them, and to work from an outline to make sure we don't miss anything. These "tips" are, for the most part, instinctive and need not be taught for an exorbitant price. Indeed, most lawyers learned them in a law school trial practice course.

I began to wonder about the backgrounds of those offering up this kind of advice, so I took a look at their backgrounds.

What I found was disappointing, but not surprising. Most authors and speakers have very little actual experience in depositions. I reached that conclusion by first searching the federal case management/electronic case filing database (CM/ECF) for cases in which they've appeared. The majority of them were identified as counsel in *fewer than fifty cases* in their entire career. Most were not involved in high-volume practices or in fields known for frequent trials. Some practice in areas where documents, not depositions, drive the outcome.

Don't believe me? Think of the most experienced litigator you can think of – someone you know, someone you've seen on TV – and search their name in the Advanced Party Search on PACER.gov. (That field retrieves lawyer appearances as well as actual party names.) You'll be shocked by the result. The fact is, most litigators just don't have deep experience.

Even in fairly large organizations with substantial numbers of trial lawyers, the skill associated with evaluating the need for, and method of conducting, depositions, is lacking. *E.g., Dalton v. Barrett,* 2019 WL 3069856, at *17 (W.D. Mo. July 12, 2019) (federal consent decree requiring training on depositions imposed where evidence showed no depositions were taken in 97% of criminal cases and lawyers lacked basic knowledge about when and how to take them).

My background is different. If you search the CM/ECF database in the two states where I practice, you'll find that I have appeared as chief counsel in more than a *thousand* federal cases.

Over my career, my practice has been roughly divided equally between federal and state courts. If I conservatively estimate, then, that I have appeared in as many state court cases as I have in federal cases, you can safely conclude that I have appeared as chief counsel in more than *two thousand* cases. My practice area is high-volume and involves many depositions. The typical case I handle involves between 10 and 25 depositions. I estimate - based on the number of cases I have handled, and the average number of depositions in each - that I have probably taken or defended in excess of 20,000 depositions over my career. The basic math supports that. I originally chose the title for this series out of sheer modesty (and have kept the reference to 10,000 because the publisher does not want me to change the series title at this point).

My goal in drafting the 490-page practitioner's master-work, *10,000 Depositions Later: The Premier Litigation Guide for Superior Deposition Practice* - from which this mini-guide was drawn - was not to add another book to the shelf about the mechanics of taking depositions. Every other book does that. My goal was to discuss strategies and tech-niques you can't find elsewhere. Over the course of thousands and thousands of depositions, I've paid attention to what works and what doesn't and made many changes, sometimes almost imperceptible, in the way I approach the examination of witnesses. Over time I learned that some of those changes routinely led to big payoffs.

Some people say that if you focus on the basics, you'll do just fine. I think the opposite. If you're not looking for oppor-tunities in the corners, where no one else is looking, if you're not looking for the micro-advantages that will make a differ-ence in the close cases, and get you across the goal line, you're missing opportunities.

How big are small advantages? Consider this, from some Wall Street traders that recognize the value of searching out every conceivable advantage. A few years ago, a trading group spent almost half a billion dollars to pay for a relatively short underground cable that would transmit trades about *three milliseconds* faster than the cables currently in place.

Three milliseconds is three one-thousandths of a second.

This uptick in speed is so absurdly small as to be imperceptible. But the traders realized that, in a highly competitive field, every conceivable advantage that can be pursued must be pursued. They scrutinized every component of the trading process and had identified even minuscule changes that could make a difference. They overlooked nothing.

This systematic approach to successful investing is the difference between amateurs and pros. Small changes often result in the biggest gains. Professionals always look in the corners for micro-advantages. Professional athletes, once they establish their basic routines, immediately begin looking for ways to improve them.

They devote enormous resources to finding advantages. It may be a slight adjustment to the way they run, the way they throw, the way they hold the bat, hold the club or kick the ball. Once they make those changes, they begin looking for a way to make that change even better. It never stops. Professionals in every occupation know that continued success demands a constant hunt for improvements.

The practice of law is no different.

Princeton University Professor Daniel Kahneman, a Nobel Prize-winning psychologist and economist, contends that the only real way to develop true expertise is to (a) engage in regular practice, and (b) have swift feedback.

But the problem is that a litigator who takes a limited number of depositions each month, and who rarely tries cases, has neither. It is thus impossible for them to try a range of techniques in heavy practice and quickly see the results. My high-volume practice allows me to engage in frequent experimentation, to see over and over the results of my tactics. I see the results after the depositions, in settlement talks, in mediations, and in trial outcomes.

This advanced guide reveals what I know works in preparing deponents for their depositions. You can use these expert-level techniques even if your deposition activity is limited. In other words, you can implement the most advanced deponent preparation strategies in the profession without the need to devote thirty years in daily litigation warfare.

Try the techniques in this guide in preparing your deponents, making your own adjustments to suit your style. If you are hesitant to implement them on a widespread basis, try them individually. You will see noticeable differences in the effectiveness of your deponents as they face the often clever, and sometimes shameless, tactics thrown at them by opposing litigators

You cannot afford to do less in preparing deponents for their depositions. The universal rule, with limited exceptions, is that a witness cannot be deposed twice. That often works to the benefit of your deponents, but it can work to their (and your) tremendous disadvantage if they performed poorly.

But there's no reason for that. Any witness, regardless of experience, can be turned into an invincible deponent if properly prepared. Use this guide, and watch the strength of your cases rise dramatically.

Jim Garrity

1

CREATING INVINCIBLE DEPONENTS - PART 1

Preparing for Examination

Covered in This Chapter:

- *§10.01 Preliminary overview*
  - *§10.02 Poor preparation destroys cases*
  - *§10.03 Bullet-proofing your witness*
  - *§10.04 The training must mirror the battle*
  - *§10.05 A witness stronger than needed*
  - *§10.06 A sample client prep session*
  - *§10.07 "Thanks for coming in."*
  - *§10.08 "You must answer every question."*
  - *§10.09 "TV depositions are not realistic."*
  - *§10.10 "The opposing lawyer is not your friend, and is not neutral.*

•*§10.33 "They'll ask about acts of dishonesty."*

•*§10.34 "You'll be asked who's helping you."*

•*§10.35 "They'll ask if you've removed data."*

•*§10.36 "They'll ask if you've recorded calls."*

•*§10.37 "They'll ask about texts, emails and social media."*

•*§10.38 "They'll ask about your medical history."*

•*§10.39 "They may ask about substance abuse."*

•*§10.40 "Some anxiety is a good sign."*

•*§10.41 "Take hourly breaks to clear your head."*

•*§10.42 "Never reveal our communications."*

•*§10.43 "Be truthful about everything."*

•*§10.44 "I am not your cheerleader."*

HERE, I focus chiefly on preparing your own clients and witnesses to have their deposition taken.

§10.01 Preliminary Overview

Because most cases never make it to trial, I urge lawyers to invest *heavily* in preparing clients and witnesses for deposition testimony. It is their performance in that arena that will power your case into the Winner's Circle.

Your opponents will use depositions not only to make judgments about the merits, but also as a gauge of the overall calibre of your clients. Are they confident? Is their testimony unequivocal? Are they easily angered? Do they exaggerate? Do they pay attention?

The presumption, sometimes correct, is that a witness' deposition performance will mirror their performance before a jury. In other words, all you see is all there is. So the value of cases tend to rise or fall in the aftermath. Thus the time you invest rendering your witnesses invincible will return dividends in multiples.

§10.02 Poor Preparation Destroys Cases

A surprising number of lawyers arrive at their offices on the day of depositions, or at the reporter's office, without having spent one moment getting their client ready. They offer the thinnest of guidance: "Tell the truth." "Pay attention." "Watch out for trick questions." "Just answer yes or no." "Don't expand on your answer."

These trite, threadbare platitudes offer clients no lifeline. *Of course* your client should pay attention. *Of course* your client should watch out for trick questions, whatever those are. *Of course* your client should tell the truth. So far, lawyers using this approach have said nothing of value. As for lawyers who tell clients not to expand on their answers, or to "just answer yes or no," it's hard to tell who has been to fewer depositions, the client or the lawyer.

Your clients will sit for hours on end; answer many different types of questions; review and testify about documents; defend and explain their answers; and fend off aggressive declarative statements, not to mention a barrage of taunts, innuendo, and hints if not accusations of misconduct or incompetence.

A deposition is a complex and lengthy intellectual sword fight. If your client's blade has not been sharpened, the ensuing contest of wills may well be disastrous.

§10.03 Bullet-Proofing Your Witness

There are three elements to best-in-class deposition preparation. You must:

Explain the process, start to finish. Explain what a deposition is, how it is used (case evaluation, summary judgment, impeachment), who reads it, who will be present and their roles, and where everyone sits. Stress that the opposing lawyer is the opposing team's coach.

Offer numerous examples of tricks and traps. Offer numerous examples of tricks and traps, with anecdotes from actual depositions. This includes tricks to lower their guard, misstatements about the case and the many forms of misleading questions.

Conduct at least two thorough, aggressive mock cross-examinations. Stay in character as the opposing lawyer, and insist your client do likewise, as the deponent. Use multiple tricks and traps. I aim for a total of five hours of mock examination, including background questions and breaks. Make your mock examination identical to the actual experience. Finally, and once you understand the ten to twenty case-critical questions that could make or break the case, ask them over and again through the deposition, slightly varying the way you ask the questions each time. Get your client used to recognizing those questions no matter how they're worded.

Your opposing number will ask them many times and in many different ways.

I generally break the preparation sessions into two days, and I do a final, highly-condensed one the morning of.

The goal is to expose clients to the approach they will face in the actual deposition. This includes introductory instructions, background questions, and documents. In general, it is not difficult to figure out most or all the questions likely to be asked, and to pose them to clients in the mock deposition session.

§10.04 The Training Must Mirror the Battle

In preparation sessions I use the style of the opposing lawyer.

If the lawyer's style is aggressive, I am aggressive.

If the lawyer is given to putting words in witness' mouth, I rely heavily on leading questions and unfavorable declarative statements.

If the opposing lawyer tends to smirk, interrupt, feign shock or disbelief during depositions, I do that as well.

Clients do best when exposed to the exact experience they will face. And I will reword questions to see if the client has absorbed the concepts, or gets confused if I ask the same thing a different way. It is great if they answer a softball question in a solid way; not so much if I rephrase the exact same question and the clients have no idea what to say.

I will also rush the clients, interrupt them, push documents in front of them or pull them back quickly, suggest that the client's testimony has been dishonest, and suggest that the client's claims or defenses are a sham.

I may use documents that have nothing to do with the case, to see if the client is even paying attention.

I want to develop the clients' range, so they can easily adapt to anything thrown at them. I also want to see if I can get the clients to admit they are speculating (especially when they are not), and agree they have no idea whatsoever whether their views have any basis in fact whatsoever (when they clearly do).

I may ask clients if they are willing to change their minds based on what other witnesses are going to say, and I then make up "mystery meat" testimony to see if the client bites or knows how to respond to supposed testimony no one has given or ever will give.

§10.05 A Witness Stronger Than Needed

When depositions of my clients start, they are ready to fight. There will be nothing asked that they cannot answer. Lawyers who interrupt my clients will find my clients talking over them until my clients have finished their answers. Lawyers who are disrespectful will hear aggressive objections from the clients. Lawyers who attempt to rush my clients through documents will be shut down.

This is how to prepare your clients. This is how you win cases through your depositions.

§10.06 A Sample Client Prep Session

Let's work through a sample deposition preparation

session for the typical client. Your client may be more or less sophisticated than this sample fits, so adapt accordingly. The approach here presumes a civil case, a client who is fairly sophisticated and understands the basic concepts, but who has never been a witness before and is generally unfamiliar with court proceedings, depositions or trials.

This is a summary. It does not include all the things I cover every time. But if you use this as a starting guide, and then develop your own preparation session from there, you will be in great shape.

§10.07 "Thanks for coming in."

What we're going to do today is get you ready to be the best possible witness you can be. Since you've never had your deposition taken before let me give you an outline or frame-work of the process. It's important to understand what a deposition is, and how it will be used.

Your deposition will be a question and answer session about all of the relevant claims and defenses in the case. It will be in a conference room just like this one. At one end of the table will be the court reporter, who is going to take down every word you say. The record created will be preserved for all of time.

Across from you will be the lawyer for the opposing side. He or she will be asking you questions. There may or may not be a representative of the company there, but don't worry. The representative cannot say anything, and cannot engage in behavior of any kind that will distract you. If they do, I will put a stop to that immediately.

he lawyer will ask you a series of questions, typically beginning with background questions about you, your education, work history, and family life. The lawyer will then turn to the facts relevant to your claims or defenses. The first segment on background issues may take an hour or two. The balance of the deposition will be about the case.

§10.08 "You must answer every question."

There are some exceptions to this, but the lawyer on the other side is solid and is not the type of lawyer who will ask wildly inappropriate questions. So whether you think the questions are relevant or not, you must answer them unless I tell you otherwise. And it is highly unlikely I will instruct you not to answer a question, so you should not look at me every time you're asked a question to see if I want you to answer it. If I do not, I will let you know.

Focus on the question and on giving your best and most accurate answer. You may have heard some people say the best way to respond to questions is with a simple yes or no, and nothing else. That is not how depositions work. Most of the questions will require you to give explanations. There will be some questions that call for a simple yes or no answer, but most will require detail.

§10.09 "TV depositions are not realistic."

If you're like most people, you've probably seen lots of

movies and TV shows about lawyers, lawsuits and courtrooms. Those shows are written for entertainment purposes, not to resemble anything that actually happens in real life. Real trials are not like TV trials. Real judges are not like TV judges. And real depositions are not like what you've seen anywhere else. They are one form of court proceeding, and they are to be conducted like that. I will not be screaming and shouting things like "This is a search for the truth!" I won't be constantly talking over the other lawyer, or telling you not to answer questions. Further, you should not look at me for signals on how to answer anything. No blinks, winks, hand gestures - nothing. Just as it would be improper for me to do that in a courtroom in front of a judge and jury, it is improper for me to do those things in your deposition. I will protect you from misconduct, but in most circumstances the lawyer's conduct will be proper, and so will his or her questions. It may not be entirely pleasant for you, but I will make sure it is within the confines of what courts allow. The purpose of our conversation right now is to get you ready. Once the deposition begins, the answers must come from you. A court would likely fine both of us, or worse, if we engaged in that kind of conduct. TV lawyers might do that, but real lawyers who want to remain lawyers do not.

§10.10 "The opposing lawyer is not your friend, and is not neutral."

Lawyers sometimes start depositions in a very friendly way, with something like "I'm just here to find out what happened."

But know this. That is not true. The only neutral participants in a lawsuit are the judge and jury. In contrast, lawyers are advocates for their client. Think of the opposing lawyer as the coach for the opposing team. I am, in turn, the coach of your team. Never confuse the role of the lawyers. We are not neutral. We are there to win. The opposing lawyers were hired to hurt your case, and they need your help. They need you to assume they're neutral, maybe even your friend. They need you to relax your guard, and to pay very little attention to what they're asking. The minute you lower your guard is the minute you start getting hurt. The opposing lawyers are there to do you damage. They have no other purpose.

§10.11 "The lawyer will try to put words in your mouth."

There are two ways that lawyers can ask questions. Let me explain both.

One style of questioning is what I call the "pull" method. This is where the lawyer frames questions to *pull* information from you. These are questions like the following: "So what did you do next? What did he say? Tell me what happened?"

The other type of examination involves what I call "push" questions.

This is a more aggressive, antagonistic form of questioning that requires you to be stay sharp and be very firm. Example: "You never made a complaint to human resources, *did you?*" "You looked away before the light turned, *didn't you?* " "You knew the content was a trade secret, *didn't you?*"

This form of question does not ask what you know. *It tells you what you supposedly know to be true and demands you agree.* You must listen with great caution to this form of examination. You must speak up if any piece of the question is inaccurate. You must never agree to an aggressive statement that is simply *close* to what you would say.

If it is not 100% correct, if it is only 99%, you must speak up and explain why it is wrong and why you do not agree.

§10.12 "Your deposition is not a practice run."

Everything you say counts. It is critical that you understand that most cases never go to trial. Most are settled, or thrown out, based on what the parties and witnesses say in depositions.

So this is not a situation where you work out the kinks in your deposition, get a feel for what's important, and then do your thing at trial. If your deposition testimony is not solid, you will never have another chance to tell your story. There will be no trial. So this is it.

§10.13 "The judge will read every word you say."

The judge will eventually get a copy of the transcript of your deposition and review every word you said. That's who matters most.

It is useful to imagine the judge is listening in on the phone as you testify. He or she won't be of course, but it's useful to think of it that way, because in a very real way, that is who you are talking to during your deposition.

If the judge reviews your transcript and thinks your testimony is weak, untruthful, unfounded or speculative, your case is over. You will never see the inside of a courtroom. This is why the opposing lawyers will be doing everything they can to confuse you, to trip you up, to get you to lower your guard, and to force admissions out of you that may not even be correct. Those lawyers know how your transcript will be used, and they will do everything they can to make sure that it is useful to them and harmful to you.

§10.14 "Here's how deposition transcripts are used."

First, this isn't a criminal case, but I'm sure you've heard the expression,"Everything you say can and will be used against you in a court of law." The same is true here. Once the deposition is over, everyone will get a transcript, a word for word account, of what you said today. And here's how they're used.

First, the opposing lawyer will try to have your case thrown out at some point down the road. In doing so, the lawyer will rely heavily on your deposition testimony - *your own words.* That's one reason why it's important to pay attention. Lawyers may even use small snippets of your testimony, present them to the judge, and use them as a basis for the court to throw your claims or defenses out. For opposing lawyers, that is a key function of your deposition - as a tool against you. Because you are a party in the lawsuit, your words matter more than most. If you offer damaging testimony, it is far more likely to hurt the case at its core than testimony offered by others that have an obvious bias against you.

Second, your deposition testimony can be read out loud to the jury at trial to make you look dishonest or incompetent. This is because opposing lawyers are allowed to tell the jury what you said in deposition if you are asked the same question at trial and give a different answer.

So if you give a different answer in court, the lawyer will hand you a copy of your deposition while you are on the stand, ask you to turn to the page that has the same question, read the question out loud, and then demand that you read your prior, *different* answer to the jury.

At that point, the jury may think you can't keep your story straight. This will cause the jury to lose faith in your truthfulness. If it happens enough - if there are multiple occasions where your answers at trial differ from what you said in deposition - the jury is likely to reject what you say and rule against you. The transcript, in other words, will be used to embarrass you, and to paint you as dishonest, if you're not careful and consistent.

In virtually all trials, juries hear two very different versions of events. They have no way to know who is right and who is wrong except by deciding who is believable and who is not. That is where deposition testimony comes in. The party that has more inconsistencies in what their witnesses say is the one that usually loses.

§10.15 "Let's talk about how to answer questions."

The basic rule of thumb is this.

Listen to the question.

Answer the question fully and completely.

Then stop.

A question that calls for a yes or no response is fully answered by a yes or no. A question that asks you to recount a conversation is fully answered when you have recounted the conversation. Once you have done that, stop. If the lawyer is pushing facts on you and asking you to agree, you must listen carefully and agree only if the assumptions in the question are 100% accurate. If they are not, you must say so.

§10.16 "A deposition is not a social conversation."

A chatty approach to answering deposition questions will get you into trouble. It is unlikely you will fully appreciate how certain questions are intended to trigger harmful answers.

For example, some questions might be tied to legal standards about which you know nothing. If you're not careful, you might give an exceedingly clever answer that literally sinks your own ship.

You must answer all questions truthfully, fully and completely, but once you have given a complete answer, stop talking. In a social conversation, if I ask whether you have children, you might answer not only by telling me yes, but also by telling me their names, how old they are, and what they are doing in life right now. In a deposition, if I ask you whether you have children, the full, complete and correct answer is "yes" or "no."

That's the approach to take. Your deposition is not the time to show how everyone smart you are, or to show how much you know. It is to answer questions put to you and, when the questions are done, to leave the room.

§10.17 "Listen to the preliminary instructions."

The lawyer questioning you will generally ask you if you are suffering from medical conditions, or taking any medications, that will affect your ability to tell the truth. The lawyer will tell you to speak up if you don't understand a question and that, unless you do, the lawyer will assume you understood it. This goes back to what I said before: if you are not sure what a question means, ask the lawyer to rephrase it.

If you answer a question without asking for clarification, the lawyer, judge and jury will assume you understood the question and you will be stuck with your answer.

§10.18 "Answer questions fully and completely."

You should not play word games or hold back information responsive to the questions. "Yes" or "No" is not a complete answer if the question calls for you to elaborate. If you fail to elaborate and provide all information called for by the question, you may not be able to use the additional information later. And if you are allowed to expand your answer in trial, the opposing parties will paint you as dishonest for not answering completely in your deposition. Juries do not like dishonest or game-playing witnesses.

§10.19 "If you don't know the answer, say so."

Do not guess. Guesses count as real answers even if they are wrong, even if you say you're guessing. And if they are wrong, they will be used against you at trial.

Here are some telltale phrases that you're derailing your case:

•*You start your answer with, "Well, I don't really know, but I'd say...."*

•*Or, "Not sure. Maybe a hundred."*

•*Or, you give a full answer, and then say, "But don't hold me to that."*

•*Or, "I can't swear to it, but...."*

I should never hear you say any of those things in your deposition. If I do, it means you are answering questions with guesses, not facts. This is how cases are lost. You are not required to guess.

Sometimes opposing lawyers will invite you to guess. For example, after you say you do not know something, the lawyer may respond immediately with "What's your best guess?" The only answer you should give after that is, "I just told you that I do not know."

§10.20 "If you don't remember something, say so."

If you knew the answer at one point but do not remember at the moment you are asked the question, you can simply say "Sitting here right now, I don't remember." The opposing lawyers might get frustrated, and might even think you are pretending not to remember. Of course, you should not pretend to suffer memory failure in response to any question.

But if you do not remember at the moment you are asked the question, that is a legitimate answer. I do not care whether the opposing lawyer thinks you remember the answer or not. I only care that you answer fully and correctly about those things you remember and that you refrain from answering when you do not remember.

§10.21 "But don't use 'I don't recall' as a crutch."

Remember this. You cannot use "I don't remember" as a crutch to avoid a question when you actually do recall the answer. Once you say "I don't remember" or "I don't know," you may be stuck with those answers for the rest of the case, including at trial.

These answers leave a hole in your case. That hole will be filled, in most circumstances, by an opposing witness who will clearly recall the answer, especially if the opponent knows you can't offer a different version of events. And their recollection will not be beneficial to you.

When a jury has to decide which version of an event to believe, and it must choose between (a) an opposing witness who gave a clear, specific answer, and (b) you, who said "I don't remember," who do you think gets the jury's vote?

Right. Our opponent.

Holes in our case created by lots of "I don't know's" and "I don't remember's" do tremendous damage. You are stuck with those answers. And it can get worse if, at trial, you suddenly have all the information that you claimed you didn't have in your deposition.

§10.22 "Never change answers under pressure."

Lawyers are generally only allowed to ask you a question

once. Do not change your answer just because the lawyer repeats the question.

Court rules generally forbid lawyers from repeatedly asking the exact same question. Doing so is almost always an effort by the lawyer to get you to change your answers. Sometimes, I see witnesses getting nervous when a lawyer repeats a question, and they actually change their answer. Such witnesses find themselves in deep trouble because they've now given two different answers to the same question (and both can be read to the jury to imply confusion or dishonesty).

You should never change your answers unless you made a legitimate mistake, which is unlikely. If I catch the lawyer repeating the same question over and over, I will speak up, and I will take steps to prevent you from being subjected to the same question again.

Indeed, some lawyers will openly press you to change answers. For example, if you say you do not remember something, the lawyer might retort, "Well, this is my only opportunity to question you before trial, so I need an answer. If you need to take a break, that's fine, but I need you to answer the question." But if you do not remember, "I don't remember" is a complete answer, and you have satisfied your obligation.

Never concoct an answer under pressure from a lawyer. Sometimes situations like this are caused by the failure of the opposing lawyers themselves. They could have easily anticipated that you might not remember an event or document from several years ago and could have provided you documents to refresh your memory, for example. Now in deposition, and having failed to construct an examination with documents to refresh your memory, the lawyer either goes away empty-handed on key questions or decides that pressuring you is a good alternative.

I cannot say it enough. Your obligation is to answer questions fully and completely at the moment you are asked them. You are not required to have a perfect memory. No one has one.

§10.23 "If you don't understand a question, say so. Say nothing else."

You should never answer a question when you are unsure what is being asked. You should only say you do not understand the question. Then stop talking and wait for a rephrased inquiry.

You may not know *why* a lawyer is asking a question, but you are entitled to understand what a specific question seeks. If you do not understand the question, say so. Then ask the lawyer to repeat it or reword it.

Never reword the question yourself, such as "Well, are you asking me [A] or are you asking me [B]?" If you reword the question, the lawyer will likely insist that you answer both the question you came up with and the lawyer's original question. That means you just turned one question into two - congratulations! - and your rephrasing might do you more harm than what the lawyer asked.

§10.24 "If the lawyer interrupts you, keep talking."

Lawyers may interrupt you if you begin offering an answer that is particularly damaging to their client. Why? A half answer counts as nothing to a judge and jury.

If you allow interruptions, the transcript will look something like this:

Q: Did he tell you the company had approved your removal of the documents?

A: He said, well, you can take the strategy papers and customer lists if you - -

Q: That's not what I asked you. I asked if he told you the company had approved your removal of the documents?

The reporter will note that you were interrupted with two dashes. But that's it. The rest of your answer is nowhere to be found.

Lawyers who use interruption as a tactic won't admit their motives. They may actually blame you, saying you weren't answering the question asked. And after cutting off your response, the lawyer may swiftly jump to another topic as a distraction, hoping you never finish your answer.

Whether your answer fairly responded to the question isn't for the lawyer to decide. You are entitled to complete your response. If the lawyer thinks your answer doesn't meet the question, he or she can try it a different way. But interruption is not proper.

Sometimes interruptions are unintentional. Often, they are not. There is no easy way to tell. So here's the rule: Never allow an opposing lawyer to interrupt you and cut off your response. Once you begin a response, finish it.

§10.25 "Do not answer until you hear the entire question."

You must let the lawyer finish his or her question before you start to answer. Just as the lawyer must allow you to finish your answers, you must allow lawyers to finish their questions. The transcript will become a mess if each of you interrupts the other.

But just as an incomplete answer is harmful to you, responding to an incomplete question can also do you harm.

Why?

Because you're likely to wrong about what was about to be asked. Sometimes answers blurted out in haste are actually worse than what the lawyer was about to ask. You must wait to hear the entire question, reflect, and then give your best and most powerful answers.

This isn't the lightning round in a game show. In this setting, speed kills.

§10.26 "Read all documents with great caution."

As I said before, all your answers count. This includes answers about documents.

All things considered, depositions proceed at a fairly swift pace. Years of events may be covered in the span of a few hours. Likewise with documents. You may be shown thousands of pages of documents in the course of a single day of testimony. Handbooks, manuals, contracts, long email chains - you name it.

And because your deposition is limited to one day of seven hours, the lawyer is likely to pass documents across the table to you without any intention whatsoever of letting you properly review them. They just want a yes or no as to its authenticity before they take it back.

You can't buy into that. If you are asked to review a document and agree to its authenticity - meaning it is a complete, unaltered version - you must go through it with great caution. Once you answer yes or no, you are bound by the answer. There's no "Well, I didn't read it" later.

In fact, the transcript will not show how long you took to review the document before you said it was a true copy. A judge and jury will assume you took all the time you needed, unless you said otherwise.

If I were shown a lengthy handbook or manual and asked to quickly agree it is authentic, I'm certain I would look at the lawyer, incredulously, and say that I must review every page before I can say so - and maybe not even then.

How can I verify a document's authenticity without time to reflect? Without comparing it to the copy I have? Without looking at every page? Without conferring with others, if need be? And if the document contains signatures, checkboxes, or handwritten notes or narratives, then quickly attesting to its authenticity *under oath* is simply impossible.

Should I just trust that the documents haven't been tinkered with? No. Nor should you. If you cannot properly review them and then give an accurate answer, you cannot attest toothier authenticity.

By the way, there is another, more appropriate way for lawyers to show you lengthy documents and ask for your agreement that they're genuine. The lawyer could send you copies and allow you thirty days to review them before you give a thumbs up or thumbs down on authenticity.)

You do not have to admit a document is authentic just because it is put in front of you. If you cannot say so, you must not say so.

§10.27 "People do alter documents, and it may not be obvious."

It is not unheard of for parties to alter documents. Be suspicious. *So you cannot assume anything.*

Parties sometimes do alter documents. It could be anyone from an entry-level employee to the CEO. Lawsuits are contentious; parties may see the act of fraudulently altering documents as an act of true justice, or even vengeance. Someone might also alter a document to protect themselves.

And changes can be subtle. Some examples:

•A handbook may be a newer version with an older cover slapped on it, suggesting it was in effect during the relevant period

•A guide may have individual pages substituted, so while the overall guide is correct, key pages are the wrong ones

•Some signatures may have been added; others might have been removed

•Boxes that were checked may now be blotted out

•Boxes that were blank may now be checked

•Email chains may be missing key responses and replies

•Documents may have been created on dates other than those shown

•Digital files may have been modified

When the stakes are high, some people will do whatever it takes to win. This is why you must be absolutely certain the document is what it claims to be before you say so. "It looks right," or "It's probably right" are not acceptable answers.

§10.28 "If you're unsure about a document's authenticity, do not take a stance on it."

If you refuse to say a document is authentic, the lawyer may try the next best thing, which is to say, "Well, do you have any basis to believe the document is *not* authentic?" This is the same question, coming in the back door.

In fact, if you were not given the time and opportunity to carefully assess a document, you have no basis even to say "Nothing stands out," because that implies some level of complete, appropriate review took place. And if you do buy into that, your answer will be portrayed like the following in court papers as if you'd said the document was genuine:

Even Mr. Hernandez admitted in his deposition that "Nothing stands out" to suggest the contract was altered in any way whatsoever.

So refrain from informal assessments of documents shown

to you in deposition, just as you must refrain from informal guesses in questions generally.

§10.29 "Opponents might have altered your documents."

Once we turn copies of our documents over to our opponents, there is a risk that someone has altered them. Thus even if you are handed copies of your own documents in deposition, you must view them as skeptically as documents created by anyone else. They are no longer *your* documents; they are *copies* of your documents that have been in the possession of your adversary.

During most lawsuits, parties exchange documents. We produce our supporting documents to them; they produce theirs to us. But once our documents are in the hands of a foe, we cannot say without review that they remain unaltered. They may have been scanned in and altered in numerous ways.

So even if you are shown copies of your own documents, exercise the same caution as if they came from a hostile party - because they just did. The lawyer may seem exasperated at your stance - "*These are your own documents!*" - but disregard the show.

All documents, once in the hands of an opponent, must be viewed with suspicion, regardless of their initial origin.

§10.30 "Some questions may be very personal."

You will be asked a series of background questions once the deposition begins. This is normal and you should answer them without flinching unless I specifically tell you not to.

Courts allow some degree of intrusion into the backgrounds of opposing parties. This ensures that, within reason, details that might shed light on the case come to light.

Initial questions may seek information about where you live, who you live with, the names of your children, how old they are, and the names of current or former spouses. I appreciate that these questions can seem like an invasion of privacy.

But here's one reason why lawyers ask about these things. They want to know if anyone related to you shows up on the jury pool or on a witness list. Even close family members may have different last names, and they want to make sure that your brother-in-law, for example, isn't chosen to sit on the jury without their knowledge.

Another reason lawyers ask about the people in your immediate family and social circles is to learn the identities of those you've probably talked to about your case. You should not be offended if you are asked for this information. You must generally provide it.

§10.31 "You'll be asked about prior cases."

The court files from other cases you've been involved in can provide a wealth of information to an adversary. (We make use of opponents' prior cases, too.)

This includes cases where you have sued others, where you have been sued, where you have filed for bankruptcy, or where you have filed for government benefits, such as unemployment compensation, Social Security Disability benefits, or workers' compensation benefits. All can provide relevant information. You should be prepared to reveal prior matters in which you were involved.

§10.32 "They'll ask about your criminal history."

Criminal histories can have some bearing on the issues in a case, depending. If you have ever been arrested, charged or convicted of a crime, tell me now. I'll decide if you should acknowledge the incidents or whether we should object.

And if you have successfully petitioned to have prior criminal histories expunged, let me know that, too.

If we decide you must answer questions about prior criminal charges, just answer the questions truthfully and completely. I will not let an opposing lawyer dig any deeper than the law allows (which generally stops at the nature of the charge and the outcome).

Sometimes lawyers ask questions like this simply to cause embarrassment. Once embarrassed, witnesses may become too distracted to perform well for the balance of the deposition.

It's just a tactic. I can assure you that everyone in the deposition room has dealt with people with every conceivable kind of criminal charge. No one cares.

Just answer the questions and move on.

§10.33 "They'll ask about acts of dishonesty."

You may be asked if anything on your resume or job application is inaccurate. Remember that *any* omissions, even of modest jobs, technically make them"inaccurate." So review your application or resume if a copy is provided you and note any omissions. If you are not provided a copy, insist on being provided a copy before you give a definitive answer.

You might also be asked whether you have engaged in any undiscovered misconduct pertinent to the case at hand. You might be asked about pending judgments or liens whether you've filed all your tax returns; whether you've accurately reported all your income; and whether ou owe child support or alimony.

Let's talk about these if you have concerns.

§10.34 "You'll be asked who's helping you."

Sometimes people employed by adversaries help my clients confidentially. They provide insights, key information, and sometimes documents we didn't know about.

You will be asked about your contacts with current or former employees. If you have, the opposing lawyers may already know about them, and are simply testing your truthfulness.

Or they may have no idea and the question is a random question.

If you've had contact with people affiliated with our opponent, let me know. "Contact" includes emails, texts phone calls - anything of substance other than "Hi" in passing at the store. Your written communications might have to be produced.

And if anyone has provided you documents or sensitive internal information, we need to discuss it. In some cases the release of internal documents can lead to criminal charges, or lawsuits alleging the theft of trade secrets or company property. And it could certainly lead to the firing of the people who passed them to you.

§10.35 "They'll ask if you've removed data."

You will be asked if you took information from the opponent's computers. You will also be asked if you've logged on remotely since your authorization was terminated. Let me know if the answer is "yes" to either question.

In many situations, doing so may be illegal and could expose you to serious civil and criminal penalties. The list of acts constituting a computer crime has been vastly expanded in the last several years. It includes unauthorized access to a system; downloading or other copying of data; forwarding information stored on the system; and damage to the "integrity" of the system. The definitions of "loss" and "damage" are very broad.

If these are concerns for us, we'll need to talk about ways we can protect you. They may include asserting the Fifth Amendment or even abandoning our claims or defenses.

§10.36 "They'll ask if you've recorded calls."

You will be asked whether you surreptitiously recorded conversations, either on the phone or in person. If you did, let's talk about it. In some states, recording a conversation or call without the consent of all participants is a serious crime. In others, only one person to a conversation need consent. If you recorded conversations, let's pin down the details, including where you and each participant was physically located at the time of the recording. This could also require assessment of your potential civil and criminal liability.

§10.37 "They'll ask about texts, emails and social media."

You will be asked whether you have used text messages, emails or social media to discuss events relating to the case and, if so, with whom. Be prepared to produce them unless they're between you and me.

Further, you must not delete anything. You should know that deleting posts or messages from your profiles generally does not eliminate them. Social media sites archive your profile data and usually have everything you ever posted, sent or received through your page. Deleting content does nothing more than show an effort by you to destroy evidence.

§10.38 "They'll ask about your medical history."

Depending on the claims and defenses, you might be asked questions about your medical condition, diagnoses, and the medications you take. That is something we should discuss in advance. In some cases, this kind of inquiry is appropriate. In others, it is not.

§10.39 "They may ask about substance abuse."

I'll provide you guidance about how to deal with this if it comes up and if your answer about prior illegal drug use will be "yes." I generally will not allow questions about drug or alcohol use or abuse, but again that is case dependent.

§10.40 "Some anxiety is a good sign."

Many clients arrive on the morning of the deposition experiencing great anxiety. Many do not sleep well the night before. Many do not eat lunch because their stomachs are in knots.

If you have some anxiety, that's a good sign, because it means you understand this is an important event. I would be more concerned if you came in this morning and told me "I've got this." *That* attitude is a sign that someone does not understand how important depositions are.

So a little nervousness and anxiety is a very good sign. We are off to a great start.

§10.41 "Take hourly breaks to clear your head."

I don't want you to get exhausted. Most deponents are slow to appreciate how exhausting prolonged examinations can be. Although it involves almost no physical activity, the stakes are high and extreme focus is required. You will get tired, whether you realize it or not.

Deponents who become exhausted do major damage to their case. Exhaustion in this setting will increase your susceptibility to influences by the examiner nd will impair your judgment and reasoning.

So you must ask for regular breaks. You need to get up, walk around, have snacks as needed and eat lunch when the time comes. Never skip breaks or meals while your deposition is in progress.

§10.42 "Never reveal our communications."

All our communications are protected by the attorney-client privilege. This means no one, including the opposing lawyer, is entitled to see our written communications or hear about our conversations.

Most lawyers will not ask questions that require you to reveal our communications, but I mention this so you do not inadvertently include conversations with me in an answer.

If any answer you give begins with "Well, I told my lawyer…" or "Well, my lawyer said….", you are revealing confidential information. Now, you might be asked questions about when you first contacted me, and other similar questions, and those might not be protected by attorney-client privilege.

Even so, you must not respond until I have had time to object or call for a recess and discuss it with you. *Motorola Sols., Inc. v. Hytera Commc'ns Corp.*, No. 17 C 1973, 2019 WL 2774126, at *2 (N.D. Ill. July 2, 2019) (noting courts have consistently held that the facts surrounding attorney-client communications, including the fact that they occurred, their dates, topics and subject matter are discoverable and not privileged, and that privilege protects only the content of communications, not underlying facts). *See also, e.g., Westhemeco Ltd. v. New Hampshire Ins. Co.*, 82 F. R. D. 702, 707 (S. D. N. Y. 1979); *Upjohn Co. v. United States*, 449 U.S. 383, 395-96 (1981); *Motorola Solutions, Inc. v. Hytera Communications Corp.*, 367 F. Supp. 3d 813, 816 (N.D. Ill. 2019).

§10.43 "Be truthful about everything."

You must never say anything in your deposition that is

untrue or misleading in any way. Even minor inaccuracies will be used to paint you as dishonest. And if it appears that you gave an answer you knew was untruthful, it could destroy your case and expose you to perjury charges.

The most important thing you can do is be honest.

You may see TV shows where lawyers encourage clients to omit facts or give false answers. That is never acceptable. And if I have ever said anything to you that you took to mean otherwise, let me assure you it is not.

In fact, I am obligated to withdraw from representation if you give false testimony. So please don't put us in that position. It is better to lose the case standing up that to win it on a bed of lies.

•§10.44 "I am not your cheerleader."

I want to make one last point. I want you to keep in mind that while I am your coach, I am not your cheerleader. I am here to win for you. I am not here to make you feel good or to pump you up just for the sake of doing so.

I do not spend much time watching sports, but I know the difference between coaches and cheerleaders. Cheerleaders cheer for their team to encourage them, to motivate them, and sometimes to entertain the audience or spectators. They play a valuable role, but it is important to understand exactly what that role is, and what it is not.

In contrast, the coach is responsible for leading training sessions, developing game plans, calling plays during the game, and making mid-game adjustments as needed to ensure victory. Coaches do not care about the spectators or about entertaining anyone. Their goal is to maximize player performance to achieve victory.

That is my role in your case, and my role in your deposition in particular. During breaks, I will be speaking with you, sometimes very firmly, about your performance up to that point. If you have not done well, I will tell you that. I will explain the mistakes you are making, and explain how you are causing damage to your own case or to the case of the organization. I will also explain tricks or tactics that I see the opposing lawyer using to weaken your testimony.

It is entirely possible that you will come out of a session during your deposition feeling that you have done extremely well when in fact you have done poorly. If that is the case, I will tell you in no uncertain terms. It is not to demoralize you. It is to encourage you to strengthen your effort, to double down, and to improve during the remaining sessions. I might very well appear upset. For that, I apologize in advance. But you will only have one shot at providing strong testimony, and I cannot afford to let that opportunity pass by suggesting your performance was better than it actually was. You should expect opposing lawyers to use every trick available to them to weaken or water down your testimony. On our end, we must likewise use every available strategy and resource to ensure that our case has improved by the time your deposition is done.

So please do not be disheartened if my comments to you

during breaks are less than positive. As long as the deposition is in progress, I have the ability to make adjustments so that your testimony is strong, clear and successful. I will not let that opportunity go. Please keep that in mind and understand that comments and guidance I provide during breaks are to ensure our mutual success, and nothing else.

THIS PAGE PURPOSELY LEFT BLANK.

CREATING INVINCIBLE DEPONENTS - PART 2

Preparing Against Trap Questions

Covered in This Chapter:

•*§11.01 Practicing for Unfair Tactics*

  •*§11.02 "But you don't actually know that, do you?"*

  •*§11.03 "So what facts do you claim to know?"*

  •*§11.04 "Tell me every fact supporting your [claim] [defense]?"*

  •*§11.05 "What if I told you Ms. Owens says she never told you that? Is she lying?"*

  •*§11.06 [Impatiently] "What is your answer? It's a simple question."*

  •*§11.07 "I don't care what you think. And I don't believe anything you're saying."*

•*§11.08 "I'm just here to find out what happened."*

•*§11.09 Questions Asserting Unprovable Facts*

•*§11.10 Influencing Testimony Through False Facts*

•*§11.11 "We've only got another hour or so. I'm about to wrap up."*

•*§11.12 "This is like a regular conversation."*

•*§11.13 "Remember, you're under oath."*

•*§11.14 "Okay. So what you're saying is…."*

•*§11.15 "I'm going to ask you again. Did you…"*

•*§11.16 "Have you ever used drugs or alcohol?"*

•*§11.17 "Did you record anything?"*

•*§11.18 "How much did your other cases settle for?"*

•*§11.19 "Have you ever filed for bankruptcy?"*

•*§11.20 "Have you ever sought Social Security benefits?"*

•*§11.21 "Did you take documents or material from the workplace?"*

•*§11.22 "Have you logged into computers or devices since your separation?"*

•*§11.23 "What did you tell your [lawyer] [accountant] [spouse] [doctor] [pastor]?"*

•*§11.24 "Do you have his number on your phone? Do you have those documents in your car?"*

•*§11.25 "Well, what would you have done if…?"*

•*§11.26 "You have other documents? Would you give them to your lawyer, so she can give them to me?"*

•*§11.27 "If you don't know, it's okay to say so."*

•§11.28 "I'm going to stand beside you and go through these documents with you."

•§11.29 "Have you now told me everything that is important about your claims?"

•§11.30 "Have you and your partner ever separated? Have you ever been unfaithful in the relationship?"

At this point we've now covered some basics to help your client become a strong witness.

In this next segment of my deposition preparations, I work through common but unfair or harassing tactics lawyers use to undermine your clients' testimony and even their confidence.

§11.01 Practicing for Unfair Tactics

It is important your clients be able to spot questions and commentary intended to adversely affect their answers and performance. These include questions that rush or pressure deponents; that are premised on false or non-existent facts; that suggest the client's answers don't amount to anything; that exhaust the client; or that require the client to apply legal principles.

So let's walk through some of the most common tricks, and talk about how to combat them. In this section, each is presented in quotes and italicized to set the tactic up as a remark made to your client during the deposition.

§11.02 "But that's just your speculation or belief. You don't know that, do you?"

This is a common problem in all lawsuits. Lawyers seek to undermine testimony by demanding that deponents admit they don't "know" something to be true. Deponents can easily become confused about the meaning of "knowing" something, and may back away from even the most obvious facts they know to be true. And that's dangerous because a deponent who is no longer sure they "know" something may abandon many of their firmly-held beliefs.

I spend some time with clients to discuss this. By the time I am done, we have eliminated this as a problem.

Opposing lawyers key in on this issue by taking the position that knowledge gained from indirect or circumstantial evidence is a nullity – that it does not count and is not "knowledge" and "knowing." Lawyers who take this approach will attempt to force your clients to admit they do not "know," and cannot claim to know, certain facts unless (a) they personally heard it, (b) they personally witnessed it, (c) the opposing party has admitted it, or (d) it was captured on audio or video.

The lawyer will press your client to admit that their perspective is something well below knowing – that it is a mere suspicion, a belief, a feeling, a thought, a speculation. If your clients buy into that, the next stop is summary judgment.

The fact is that most of what we "know" and what we deem our "knowledge" is pieced together using information from a variety of sources. That is how life works.

Most of our knowledge does not come from a direct source, from an event we personally witnessed, from a confession. We operate almost entirely on knowledge we gain indirectly or circumstantially.

But some lawyers treat the deposition room as an alternate universe, where a person knows nothing that wasn't personally heard or observed. If your clients buy into this fallacy, you are in trouble, because from there it is a slippery slope to testimony from your clients that their views are pure speculation.

So you must prepare your clients to stand their ground, whether their knowledge and knowing come from circumstantial or direct evidence. In fact, this is how our judicial system works. Evidence can be direct or indirect.

Both count equally.

Federal pattern jury instructions inform jurors that as far as the law is concerned, it makes no difference whether evidence is direct or indirect. The jury can make its decision based on either. Put another way, jurors can and will "know" something to be true regardless of how the evidence was presented. And it will make a decisive finding – guilty or not, liable or not - based on that evidence.

This is so even though the jury has not personally witnessed or personally "known" anything. The very lawyers that tell your clients they do not "know" a particular fact to be true would probably say the same thing to a jury if they could. ("You don't know! You weren't there!") But they cannot, because that is not how the system works. And, to our point here, they cannot do that in a deposition because the same principles apply to evidence in a deposition as they do at trial.

So how best to prepare your clients against lawyers who assert that because your client's knowledge or position is based on indirect evidence, your client cannot testify that what they know is anything more than a wild guess?

I usually start by outlining this problem in broad terms for clients. I explain that the opposing lawyer is likely to challenge their knowledge about certain events if the knowledge comes circumstantially. But, I say, in court proceedings, as in real life, people legitimately "know" something even if the underlying basis for their knowledge is indirect or circumstantial. In other words, circumstance-derived knowledge counts the same as first-hand-derived knowledge: video proof, confessions, and direct observation.

I often quote the following passage to clients. It's drawn from the Eleventh Circuit Court of Appeals pattern instruction and perfectly illustrates the point:

Some evidence may prove a fact indirectly. Let's say a witness saw wet grass outside and people walking into the courthouse carrying wet umbrellas. This may be indirect evidence that it rained, even though the witness didn't personally see it rain. Indirect evidence like this is also called "circumstantial evidence" – simply a chain of circumstances that likely proves a fact. As far as the law is concerned, it makes no difference whether evidence is direct or indirect. You may choose to believe or disbelieve either kind. Your job is to give each piece of evidence whatever weight you think it deserves.

So I help clients understand they can firmly testify they "know" something to be absolutely true by explaining the jury process and how juries also "know" facts with similar, absolute certainty. The umbrella example above is a good start.

I will sometimes also discuss the different burden-of-proof standards juries use.

The one all juries know is "beyond a reasonable doubt." I tell them to consider that the the 99%-certain standard.

I then talk about the "clear and convincing evidence" standard, which I loosely describe as the 66 2/3%-certain standard.

Finally, I describe the common civil standard of "preponderance" or "greater weight of the evidence," which I loosely describe as the 51%-certain standard.1 I tell my clients that under this standard, a jury can doubt *almost half my evidence* – up to 49.999999% - and still reach a concrete, unqualified determination that they know which side is right.

I may also show them a sample verdict form to end all doubt in their ability to speak in absolutist terms about what they "know." Verdict forms are black and white; they contain no shades of gray. No jury checks a box that says "WE THE JURY *feel* the defendant is guilty." No juror has personal knowledge of anything they decided, I say, but they know who wins, who loses, who goes to prison and who goes home.

The point I impress upon clients is that the judicial system allows for doubt and uncertainty, allows for knowledge based on circumstance, and does not demand scientific proof or confessions of anything in order for judges and juries to know what is true and what isn't. Certainly, scientific proof is sometimes used, and is sometimes helpful. It is not required.

And clients should use the same approach.

Thus, I explain, the notion pushed by opposing lawyers that clients need some kind of scientific proof before they "know" something is misguided, and clients should reject it. They can say they know something to be true whether their knowledge is direct or indirect.

Taking this a step further, I talk to clients about what I call "wobble words." Wobble words convey a lack of confidence about what someone knows is true. Examples include *believe, think, suspect, feel,* and *speculate.* I explain that when judges are reviewing deposition testimony, they look for wobble words. Their presence tells the judge that the deponents weren't sure about their testimony.

I conclude by saying that if the client knows something to be true, based on direct or indirect evidence that likely proves the fact, it is perfectly acceptable to say they know that fact to be true, as in, "Yes, I *do* know that," or "That *is* what happened," or "They *did* discriminate," or "They *were* negligent," or "They *did* misappropriate our customer lists," rather than the wobble-word versions "I *think* that's what happened," "I *feel* like that's what happened," or "I *suspect* that's what happened."

Game, set, match for folks who answer that way.

Indeed, testimony infected by wobble words kinds accounts for the high summary judgment rate in civil cases. Many excellent cases are lost based on deposition examinations that were crafted to walk witnesses back from what they know. You and I have both seen dispositive motions that seize on this kind of testimony to argue that the party has no evidence whatsoever to support their position (*e.g.,* "Ms. Holloman admitted in her deposition that she does not know whether this is true or not. At best, she thinks/feel/speculates that it might be.")

So we work through that until clients are comfortable with the phraseology. But I caution them that even if they do not use wobble words, opposing lawyers may forcibly inject them into the examination:

•Q: I understand that's what you *feel,* but you don't have any *proof,* do you?

•Q: But that's your *speculation,* correct?

•Q: That's what you *believe,* but you don't *know* that to be true, do you?

•Q: Well, you just told me you didn't hear that first-hand, so you actually *don't know it to be true,* do you?

There are a dozen variations of this line of questioning. They're all premised on the hoax that indirect evidence is worthless - that only direct evidence counts.

I know of no field of law in our legal system that rejects indirect evidence as a basis for knowing something. In my judgment, this type of examination is gravely misleading because it implies, if not outright asserts, that only direct evidence can support knowledge and knowing.

Clients go into depositions fully aware that this line of attack is intended to undermine and weaken their testimony.

When lawyers inject wobble words into the dialogue, clients push back: "It's not what I *feel. That's what happened,*" or, "It's not what I *think. That's why they did it.*"

By the way, many courts have said that words like "proof" and "evidence" require legal analysis and are for judges and lawyers, not for witnesses. I object when a lawyer asks a client what "proof" or "evidence" the client has to support their claims or knowledge. (These are sometimes referred to as 'legal contentions.') Lay witnesses do not know what constitutes "proof" or "evidence." The better question is to ask a witness what *information* they have upon which they base their knowledge. Then the lawyers and judge can hash out whether the information is proof or evidence.

§11.03 "So what 'facts' do you claim to "know"?

Once the issue of "knowledge" is resolved, it helps to next teach clients how to explain the *basis* for their knowledge - the underlying facts that, when strung together like beads on a necklace, constitute their knowledge.

This is straightforward. The client should testify about what they saw, heard, and read, that led them to their knowledge and knowing.

I describe this as "eyes and ears evidence." That is circumstantial evidence: information seen and heard that tends to prove a fact. If I am upstairs at home, hear the cookie jar crash, and race downstairs to see my son standing in the middle of the broken ceramic pieces - with chocolate around his mouth and, further, knowing no one else is home - I "know" with absolute certainty he is guilty. I witnessed nothing. He confessed nothing. But I know it to be true.

Our hypothetical opposing lawyer would make the claim that while I *feel, believe, suspect* and *speculate* it was him, I don't actually *know* it. Maybe the jar was already on the edge of the counter and a pet or vibration of some kind caused it to slip off.

Right.

Yet this is precisely how some lawyers approach obvious truths. They seek to subvert your case by zeroing in on knowledge gained circumstantially, sometimes while offering up other explanations that sound plausible but have no basis.

I suggest to clients that they construct their "knowledge inventory" by writing down each and every fact - document, conversation, event, policy - that led them to absolute certainty.

For example, if a 65-year old female client in an employment discrimination case believes she was passed over for promotion because of age, she should build a list like the one below to prove she knows age was a determinative factor. I encourage clients to work hard to break their knowledge down to its smallest component parts, because obvious but ultra-basic elements - such as her own age - might be seen as understood and omitted from the list.

It might look like this:

1. Her own age - 65

2. The winning candidate's age – 31

3.The ages of the hiring panel – 22, 34 and 31

4.The ages of others who were granted interviews: 22, 24, 28, 31 and 33

5.Language in the job announcement: "Looking for fresh blood"

6.Stereotyping questions during the interview: "Are you sure you can use a computer?"

7.Stereotyping comments during the interview: "I see you've got typing experience, but our concern is that things have changed since you were in high school."

8.The ages of other employees already in the same position: 23, 24, 24, 26, 27 and 35.

9.Photos of promotional brochures about the unit, depicting nothing but very young people

10.The industry segment of the employer (e.g., clothing for millennials)

11.The complete lack of other employees in any position above the age of 40

12.Her credentials versus the winning candidate: 20 years' experience versus 2

This type of list could go on and on. But all of it is based on things she saw, read or heard. No one said, "We are going to hire someone young and we will not hire you because you are old." But she can say with absolute certainty, "I *know* I was passed over because of age discrimination," and that she *knows*, without doubt, her age was the decisive factor.

It is a useful technique where the knowledge is circumstantial to force your clients to make a physical list of the underlying facts supporting their "knowing." This exercise helps them become fluid in articulating the individual components of their case. It must be done before you conduct your first mock cross-examination so your client can practice verbalizing their facts.

The actual deposition should never be the first time your client verbally recites their listed items. It won't work. If they don't practice ahead of time, they will fail to detail even a fraction of the facts contributing to their knowledge.

You might have to help them do this. You should not spoon-feed them winning examples from other cases and urge your client to simply adopt them. Start with a conversation and illustrate how intuitive knowledge can be cataloged or broken down. Without your guidance, the client may not even appreciate the incredible number of facts they already know that support their claim.

So have them make a list. Try a few light, informal practice runs where you quiz them about the facts supporting their claims or defenses.

If they struggle to come up with more than a few, try my approach. I tell clients to imagine a necklace that has no beads on it. The bare strand represents their basic claim or defense, with no facts added. Each bead is one supporting fact. I tell them they must sell their necklace to a judge and jury, but that a necklace with just two or three beads is unsaleable - no judge or jury will buy it. They must fill the strand. A full necklace contains 25, 50, whatever number of beads - individual, concrete, logical, specific facts - and every empty spot makes the necklace less likely to sell.

Interestingly, the number of fact beads I say constitutes a full necklace will heavily influence the number they end up with. For reasons that are unclear to me, if you ask someone to come up with five reasons a customer should buy a product, they struggle to come up with two or three. If you ask the same person for fifteen reasons, they 'll now easily come up with ten, but struggle to think of five more. If you ask them for fifty reasons, they hit twenty-five quickly and then start struggling.

I don't know why this is. But I have seen it my entire life. So if you want your client to come up with as many facts as possible to offer in deposition, pick a number substantially higher than you need and tell your client to hit that target. Give them a few examples to get started, and then let them do their thing.

You should also explain the basic elements of the claim. I recommend reading the pertinent pattern jury instructions to your clients, so they hear exactly what the jury will be told. Some lawyers think of jury instructions as something for juries - correct - but they're also a phenomenal tool for clients. I begin talking about the core substantive instructions in my first meetings with clients.

Instructions are perfect because they're written for laypeople. A great deal of effort goes into making them both precise and very easy to understand. Once clients know what the jury is looking for, they can make sure they provide it.

§11.04 "Tell me every fact supporting your [claim] [defense]"

This kind of question – typically referred to a legal contention - is often asked in depositions, but improperly so. *Rifkind v. Superior Court*, 22 Cal. App. 4th 1255, 1259, 27 Cal. Rptr. 2d 822, 824 (1994) ("What authority there is almost uniformly condemns the practice"); *Charal Patterson v. Department of Corrections,* Order Denying Motion for Reconsideration, CM/ECF Doc. 111, Case No. 1:12-cv-00029-MW-GRJ (N.D. Fla. Apr. 1, 2014) ("Plaintiff is not bound by answers to legal contention questions put to her during her deposition. In the first place, it is unfair to ask such questions to a layperson"); *see also Bret Schyvincht v. Menard, Inc., d/b/a Menards,* No. 18-CV-50286, 2019 WL 3002961 (N.D. Ill. July 10, 2019) (same); *Miller v. Peter Thomas Roth LLC*, No. C 19-00698 WHA, 2019 WL 3817857, at *2 (N.D. Cal. Aug. 14, 2019) (Order noting that noted it is normally improper to ask for FRCP 30(b)(6) depo-nents to testify concerning the entire basis of a claim or defense).

Legal contention questions call on the deponent, almost always a lay witness, to figure out which facts go with which legal claim or defense. Courts have said that *contention inter-rogatories* are appropriate because lawyers help clients craft those answers. But *contention deposition questions* are inappropriate because the obligation to conduct the legal analysis falls solely on the lay deponent.

From the *Rifkind* case, above:

As one commentator put it, legal contention questions require the party interrogated to make a "law-to-fact application that is beyond the competence of most lay persons." (1 Hogan, Modern California Discovery (4th ed. 1988) § 5.9, p. 252.) Even if such questions may be characterized as not calling for a legal opinion (see *Singer v. Superior Court, supra,* 54 Cal. 2d at p. 326, 5 Cal. Rptr. 697, 353 P. 2d 305), or as presenting a mixed question of law and fact (see 4A Moore's Federal Practice (2d ed.) § 33.17[2], p. 33–85), their basic vice when used at a deposition is that they are unfair. They call upon the deponent to sort out the factual material in the case according to specific legal contentions, and to do this by memory and on the spot. There is no legitimate reason to put the deponent to that exercise. If the deposing party wants to know facts, it can ask for facts; if it wants to know what the adverse party is contending, or how it rationalizes the facts as supporting a contention, it may ask that question in an interrogatory. The party answering the interrogatory may then, with aid of counsel, apply the legal reasoning involved in marshaling the facts relied upon for each of its contentions.

That, we believe, is a principal basis of the Supreme Court's dicta in *Pember II,* and of the federal authorities. It is a major reason why, as Professor Hogan puts it, "[t]aking the oral deposition of the adverse party is neither a satisfactory nor a proper way to satisfy" the interrogating party's desire to learn which facts a party thinks support its specific contentions.

§11.05 "What if I told you Ms. Owens says she never told you that? Is she lying?"

I caution clients to watch out for questions that include commentary about what other witnesses have purportedly said.

It is not proper to ask deponents what they think about the testimony of other witnesses. *See Smith v. Crews*, No. 3:12CV326/LC/CJK, 2014 WL 1900695, at *14 (N.D. Fla. May 13, 2014), *aff'd sub nom. Smith v. Sec'y, Fla. Dep't of Corr.*, 626 F. App'x 246 (11th Cir. 2015).

In fact, this kind of testy exchange is so common in depositions that I am including a quote from the state appellate decision upon which the federal judge in the *Smith/Crews* case, above relied. This is from *Boatwright v. State*, 452 So. 2d 666, 668 (Fla. Dist. Ct. App. 1984):

A second prosecutorial tactic also demands comment. During cross-examination of a key defense witness, the prosecutor skillfully established the differences between the witness's testimony and that of earlier state witnesses. Up to this point, the cross-examination was perfectly legitimate. Then, over defense objection, the prosecutor asked the witness whether each of the earlier witnesses had been lying. This effort to isolate and thereby discredit the witness is improper for a number of reasons. It is elemental in our system of jurisprudence that the jury is the sole arbiter of the credibility of witnesses. *Barnes v. State,* 93 So.2d 863 (Fla.1957). Thus, it is an invasion of the jury's exclusive province for one witness to offer his personal view on the credibility of a fellow witness. *Bowles v. State,* 381 So.2d 326 (Fla. 5th DCA 1980). Moreover, the fact that two witnesses disagree does not necessarily establish that one is lying. Lying is the making of a false statement with intent to deceive. Absent some evidence showing that the witness is privy to the thought processes of the other, the first witness is not competent to pass on the other's state of mind. Therefore, we hold that this part of the prosecutor's cross-examination was improper; the trial court erred in failing to sustain the defendant's objection.

The best approach a client can take is to decline invitations to comment on other witness' testimony. There is no basis for it. A client would not have an answer. It is not admissible. It might be reversible error to even attempt the admission of such a question an answer.

§11.06 [Impatiently] "What is your answer? It's a simple question."

Some lawyers seemingly attempt to conduct depositions of opposing witnesses at high speed. They ask questions at break-neck speed, and demand equally-swift answers. That usually isn't to save time. It is to create mental chaos for the witness.

I urge clients to pace their answers according to their need to evaluate questions before responding. Even seemingly simple questions may have nuances. Deponents get one chance to answer each question. They must get it right.

There is no bright-line rule about how long deponents should take, after a question is asked, before answering. Anecdotally, most seem to take between two and five seconds. You might practice a sample examination with your clients, using a stopwatch or app that displays seconds, to help them develop a pace that works for them.

This is not to teach them to slow festivities to a crawl. It is to teach them the value of paying close attention.

Some reflection is appropriate. Inaccurate sworn testimony has consequences. Clients must be told that answering questions quickly might seem impressive, but that is not the goal, and it is not desirable.

Fast answers are often wrong answers. Speed kills. Let them know it is okay to pause before responding. Tell them the opposing lawyer has no place telling them to answer questions more quickly. The opposing lawyer is entitled to ask questions and is entitled to straightforward complete answers. They are entitled to nothing else.

§11.07 "I don't care what you think. And I don't believe anything you're saying."

Commentary by an opposing lawyer on your client's testimony is clearly improper. And you should never tolerate an adversary who is aggressively disrespectful to your client.

Remember the core principle of Rule 30(c): "The examination and cross-examination of the deponent proceed as they would at trial…" While judges will allow an aggressive examination of a witness on the stand, they will not tolerate disrespect, taunts or insults toward the witness. There is a difference. Can you imagine a state or federal judge's reaction if a lawyer examining a witness during trial said that?

You will likely know the opposing lawyer, and his or her style of examination. In my specialized field, I generally run into the same twenty or thirty lawyers. I know who will conduct a respectful examination, who will be aggressive, and who will be disrespectful and demeaning. Where appropriate, I will talk to my client about the opposing lawyer's reputation and style, and the best way to deal with it.

I urge clients to remain professional and respectful but to speak up if they feel the opposing lawyer is treating them in a demeaning way. For my part, I will not tolerate more than a question or two that I feel is truly unprofessional before I have a dialogue with the lawyer. Whether I terminate the deposition or continue is situation-dependent, but I will not allow a deposition to proceed with a lawyer that continues to be abusive or disrespectful. Abuse affects outcomes.

Our clients can quickly become exhausted from exposure to degrading examination tactics, and it is our job to shield them and to seek court relief if it continues. While I am very slow to terminate depositions, I will do so if I feel an abusive environment is affecting the quality of the testimony. But I always engage the opposing lawyer in dialogue about their conduct before doing so.

§11.08 "I'm just here to find out what happened."

I've covered this elsewhere in the book. It is important during prep sessions to outline the roles of each deposition participant. Make sure your clients know lawyers are not neutral. They are the front-line warriors for their side, and they are there to do harm . I routinely explain the role of lawyers, judges, and juries to my clients. That way, they do not lower their guard when an opposing lawyer comes in, shakes their hand, smiles, and acts like their best friend. Even so, I have clients from time to time who buy into an opposing lawyer's charitable façade, at least until that charming lawyer starts to show his or her fangs So be sure your clients know why the opposing lawyers sit on the other side of the table. They are figuratively and literally opposite your client in every way.

§11.09 Questions Asserting Unprovable Facts

This section deals with cross-examinations about facts opposing lawyers cannot independently prove. They have a hunch that something is true (or need it to be true) but cannot establish it as a fact unless your client admits it.

Getting that admission usually depends on the lawyer's use of (a) a fast-paced examination and (b) a forceful tone of voice. Both are intended to short-circuit your client's thought process and result in swift agreement.

Some examples:

•To a deponent who did not receive a manual, *"You received a copy of this manual, correct?"*

•To a deponent never trained on reporting harassment,

"The supervisors trained you during orientation about how to report harassment, right?"

•To a deponent never trained on heavy equipment, *"You were taught how to operate the front-end loader on soft soil, right?"*

•To an employee who never received the handbook, *"You know the handbook forbids that kind of conduct, true?"*

•To an employee never told about the ethics hotline, *'You were trained to call the ethics hotline if you believed there was a problem, right?"*

Often the questions involve ordinary matters that sure sound like they'd be true. But maybe they aren't *here.*

I mean, who isn't told about company hotlines? (Many employees.) Who doesn't get a handbook? (Quite a few.) Who isn't properly trained on everything the checklist says will be covered. (Same.) With the passage of time, though, we forget the mundane. Lawyers know that and will try to patch holes in your client's memory through the power of suggestion. Without your preparation, client recollections may very well be what should have happened, not what did happen.

So it's important to educate clients about this tactic.

Stress that lawyers don't always know if assumptions in their questions are true. The rules allow them to make assumptions and demand your client admit them, though, because (the reasoning goes) a deponent will not admit something that did not happen. Lawyers only need a good-faith foundation for making assumptions, and that foundation can be very thin. For example, a random manager might have said offhandedly, "Pretty much everyone gets the handbooks and training." That could provide the basis even if, upon further inquiry, the lawyer would have learned that the manager knew of lots of examples where employees did not receive either.

It is always up to your client to determine if assumptions in questions are true, and to answer accordingly. This is a point worth repeating during prep sessions.

Their skepticism should be dialed all the way up. They must use their own judgment in responding to questions based on assumed facts. If your clients are not cautious, there is genuine risk they will admit to plausible-sounding, but entirely fictitious, events.

This is another situation where a mock cross-examination session is invaluable. Test your client's fortitude by rapidly and forcefully making declarative statements like those above, and ending with words like " ....correct?" and ".......isn't that true, ma'am?" See how often your client admits to things you know are untrue or never happened merely from the sheer force of your insistence and the seemingly-plausible nature of the assertion.

Tell clients the same thing judges tell juries: what lawyers say is not evidence. Your clients must learn to testify from their own knowledge and memory, and not from the facts your adversary is attempting to force-feed them.

§11.10 Influencing Testimony Through False Facts

Can a lawyer falsely represent (or imply) facts to your

client - such as "There are tapes of that conversation, just so you know" - as a tactic to encourage the witness to be truthful? The short answer is that knowingly making false representations of material fact to a witness during a deposition might trigger serious disciplinary charges against the attorney.

On rare occasions, you may encounter lawyers who make a show of placing a carefully marked folder or binder in front of your client before beginning a line of examination. The item suggests the lawyer has evidence regarding the questions that come next. You have no reason to believe such items exist, but there they are – or seem to be - and your client takes note.

I know of only a few occasions when lawyers have gone as far as creating folders or other items to falsely imply to the deponent that certain evidence exists and that the deponent had better not lie.

In *Cincinnati Bar Assn. v. Statzer*, 800 N.E. 2d 1117 (Oh. Sup Ct 2003), a lawyer allegedly placed a bogus, and bogusly-labeled, stack of cassette tapes on the table in front of the deponent. The purpose was to suggest the witness shouldn't lie because there were actual recordings of conversations to prove otherwise. But there weren't.

The Ohio Supreme Court, in reviewing the bar's recommended discipline, looked at it as an integrity-of-proceedings issue. The lawyer argued there was a legitimate reason for the bluff. Here's a blurb and the court's response:

Here the Respondent, however, urges us to distinguish trial

conduct from "discovery depositions," arguing that the latter require greater freedom of inquiry into matters that may be relevant but inadmissible. See Civ. R. 26(B)(1) (inadmissible evidence reasonably calculated to lead to the discovery of admissible evidence is also discoverable). This was particularly the case, respondent insists, in the deposition of the legal assistant. She argues that wide latitude was imperative during that proceeding to draw honest testimony from a theretofore untrustworthy witness and that use of the audio cassette tapes was merely a tactic intended to achieve this legitimate end. We recognize that the discovery process, particularly the pursuit of information through deposition, cannot be overly restricted if it is to remain effective. We must draw the line, however, when an attorney engages in subterfuge that intimidates a witness. While respondent's primary purpose during the legal assistant's deposition may have been to elicit the truth, her tactic also tricked the legal assistant into thinking that the revelation of embarrassing confidences was at stake.

"Throughout these proceedings, respondent has asserted that her "bluff" worked. Regardless, the success of her tactic is not at issue, and respondent can not, with any degree of certainty, assert that her witness would not have testified truthfully in the absence of her subterfuge. Further, while such deception may induce truthful testimony, it is just as likely to elicit lies if a witness believes that lies will offer security from the false threat. Respondent's deceitful tactic intimidated her witness by creating the false impression that respondent possessed compromising personal information that she could offer as evidence. For these reasons, we agree that respondent violated DR 1–102(A)(4) and 7–106(C)(1).

The lesson to be learned is that misrepresentations, verbal or demonstrative, are improper. It might be fine in a law enforcement interrogation, where bluffing can be taken to the extreme, but not in court proceedings. If you suspect the opposing counsel is using phony props during the deposition, raise the concern on the record, demand the lawyer preserve the items, consider photographing them as a precaution, and then seek court relief, either on the spot or immediately after the deposition ends.

§11.11 "We've only got another hour or so. I'm about to wrap up."

I once heard former Navy SEAL commander Jocko Willink say that one way instructors test the mental toughness of recruits is by falsely telling them they're going on a three-mile jog. At the three-mile mark, the recruits are told there was a mistake; it is actually a four-mile run. Many loud groans are heard. As recruits cross what they now think is the real finish line, they're immediately told another mistake has been made. This time, though, they're told to keep running. No promises of the end.

In fact, the real stopping point is just another half-mile - far enough past the last false finish line to test the recruits' mental resolve. Some drop out at the false finish lines. They burned all their mental energy zeroing into phantom goal lines.

As the expected end came and went, they couldn't reorient and muster more energy. They were done.

This kind of thing happens daily in many workplaces. For example, office workers may be told on a Friday at 9:00 AM that they can leave for the day as soon as they process a stack of forms. Everyone races through. The mood is super positive. At 11:00 AM, the stack is done and the cheering begins. Then, someone discovers more stacks on a back shelf. *Instantly,* the air is sucked out of the room. Defeatism rules. The mood is terrible and remains so even if the workers still leave by early afternoon. They were so fixated on a single endpoint that they couldn't adjust.

So tell your clients to plan on a very long day. Set the duration higher than the deposition could ever go. Caution them about false wrapping-up points. You might even tell them that lawyers often declare "I'm just about done" *four or five times* before it actually ends. With that knowledge, you're insulating your clients against those false goal lines.

§11.12 "This is like a regular conversation."

Depositions aren't anything like a regular conversation.

Sometimes lawyers tell deponents during preliminary instructions to think of the experience as a conversation. I'm sure many say this in good faith to help the deponent relax.

But it's important to let clients know that it is nothing like a regular conversation. Regular conversations are not under oath. Regular conversations do not involve high stakes. No one hires a lawyer to have a regular conversation. So I tell clients that while depositions have some elements of a conversation, they should not view it so informally. They should see it as a critical event.

§11.13 "Remember, you're under oath."

Some lawyers will repeatedly remind your clients they're under oath. I consider this a form of witness intimidation. It strongly implies the witness has lied, is lying, or is expected to lie, and that there are severe consequences for an incorrect answer. If it occurs more than twice, ask the examiner to refrain from further reminders. Your clients should not be laboring under a fear of being charged with perjury.

§11.14 "Okay. So what you're saying is...."

It is wise to caution clients about lawyers who summarize or rephrase their answers. The recasting is likely to be a less favorable variant of what your client just said.

Examples:

A: I was talking to my daughter about her outfit and had just dropped my bag when I turned around, looked up and saw your client run the red light.

Q: So what you're really saying is that you had an awful lot going on and you just happened to catch a glimpse of the intersection.

A: AFTER I REJECTED MY BOSS' advances, he would constantly complain about my timesheets, ignore me in meetings, and reject my suggestions.

Q: So what you're saying is that you disagree with his management style.

Summarized testimony becomes your client's testimony unless your client insists their answer remains the only answer. In the first example, the reworked summary suggests the witness' account is unreliable. In the second, it converts what might be a sexual harassment retaliation case into a non-actionable, ordinary disagreement between subordinate and supervisor.

Your clients may not realize what the lawyer is doing. One reason is that this is common in social conversations. Our family and friends often rephrase what we say, and we think nothing of it. Thus rephrasings in depositions are not likely to trigger alarm bells because it is an ordinary conversational experience.

Precisely because this tactic may seem innocent, you should educate clients about it. It may seem like the lawyer is trying to help. Stress that if the opposing lawyer restates what they say, they must firmly repeat their answer exactly as they gave it, or simply say that their answer is their answer, not what the lawyer just said.

§11.15 "I'm going to ask you again. Did you…"

Often an opposing lawyer will repeat questions previously asked and answered. It may be that the lawyer believes your client did not fully answer the question. Or it may be that the lawyer did not like the first answer and is angling for something more favorable. The solution is to listen carefully to the examination and to use your judgment in determining whether repetitious questions are improper.

There is no specific rule that forbids asking the same question more than once. The reason is that there are simply too many circumstances where asking a question more than once might be necessary to get a full and complete response. Here's what one court said about that:

In passing, the court must note that it would not be appropriate for counsel examining a deponent to repeatedly and deliberately duplicate questions previously asked by other counsel. Such a practice, although not shown to have occurred in this instance, could support a motion to terminate a deposition under Rule 30(d), if employed to such an extent that bad faith or a motive to harass the deponent could properly be inferred.

At the same time, however, an oral deposition is not merely a device to uncover and develop information. It also provides a legitimate and efficient means of testing a witness' knowledge, recollection and veracity. To these ends, counsel should be free to follow-up and explore the same subject matter covered during a previous examination, especially where the deponent's earlier responses were evasive, equivocal, or inconsistent with other testimony or evidence.

Smith v. Logansport Cmty. Sch. Corp., 139 F.R.D. 637, 646 (N.D. Ind. 1991)

Note that instructing a deponent not to answer a question because it has already been asked is typically improper. Rule

30(d) informs that you may instruct a deponent not to answer only when necessary to preserve a privilege, to enforce a limitation ordered by the court, or to present a motion under Rule 30(d)(3). That rule authorizes you to terminate or limit the deposition on the ground that it is being conducted in bad faith or in a manner that unreasonably annoys, embarrasses, or oppresses the deponent or party.

Occasional repetitious questions, therefore, provide no basis for a Rule 30(d) instruction. *Gall v. St. Elizabeth Med. Ctr.*, 130 F.R.D. 85, 87 (S.D. Ohio 1990) ("The fact that a question is repetitive is not an appropriate ground for instructing a witness not to answer a question, since it does not involve a matter of privilege"); *Smith v. Logansport Cmty. Sch. Corp.*, 139 F.R.D. 637, 647 (N.D. Ind. 1991) ("The action of plaintiffs' counsel in directing Langley and Smith not to answer certain questions on the ground that they were repetitive was clearly inappropriate.")

On the other hand, if the repetition reaches the point where you believe the examination is abusive or harassing, you have the authority to orally move for a protective order on the record, suspend the deposition, and then immediately seek court relief under Rule 30(d)(3).

§11.16 "Have you ever used drugs or alcohol?"

There are situations where this is a legitimate question. But they are few and far between.

Depending on your case, the topic of past drug, alcohol or other substance use might be something you've already discussed with your client. If necessary, tell your clients that if the question is asked, they should pause to allow you to assert the proper objections. That could be to instruct them not to answer because the question serves no purpose but to annoy, embarrass or oppress them. Remember that if you do this, you must immediately file a motion for a protective order and seek a court ruling.

§11.17 "Did you record anything?"

I presume that in doing your own due diligence, you asked whether your client has video or audio recordings of conversations or other events. It's important because some states criminalize nonconsensual recordings depending on the circumstances.

For example, some states make it a felony to record conversations or calls unless at least one participant consents. So if I am in a conversation with others, and I am taping the call, I satisfy the one-party consent requirement because I am obviously one party to the call. Some states require the consent of all participants. There may be further twists. For example, when participants on a phone call are in multiple states, which state's law determines the legality of the recording?

These laws typically require proof the participants had a reasonable expectation of privacy in the conversation. This means recording conversations in a crowded restaurant isn't likely to result in charges, whereas doing the same thing in a private passenger car might.

And there may be other exceptions. Some courts hold that recordings of conversations in the workplace are not illegal, for example, because no one in a workplace can claim a reasonable expectation of privacy in their conversations.

Whether recordings expose your client to criminal liability depends on the facts. But you must ask during your preparation session (if you've not already inquired). So many people carry recording devices these days that it's a certainty that some clients have done so. Once you learn recordings were made, you must determine whether your client should seek criminal counsel and/or assert the Fifth Amendment privilege.

§11.18 "How much did your other cases settle for?"

Most settlement agreements contain confidentiality clauses. Those clauses usually impose penalties to punish unauthorized disclosures of their terms.

If your client has previously settled a judicial or administrative dispute, he or she needs to know the risks of revealing anything about the settlement. Many lawyers ask about prior case outcomes. You should advise your client in advance of the deposition how to handle this.

An instruction not to answer may be appropriate under Rule 30(c)(2) if, at the conclusion of the prior lawsuit, a court entered an order directing the parties to comply with the terms of the agreement. This is a good reason to ask courts to order parties to comply with the settlement agreement as a final ruling in a case. That becomes the foundation for seeing relief under Rule 30(d)(3) because doing so is to "enforce a limit ordered by the court," which is language straight from the rule broad enough to cover your situation.

You may also move to terminate or limit the deposition if the inquiry meets the test of bad faith, annoyance or harassment.

Unless I can conclusively determine that testimony about a prior settlement is permitted, I do not allow clients to discuss them. Further, the outcome of a prior lawsuit rarely informs issues in a subsequent, pending case.

In some states, settlements with government entities enjoy no such protection. Where that is the case, your client will have to answer the question. Florida, for example, passed a law forbidding confidentiality clauses in settlement agreements, on the ground that the public should know how their tax dollars are being used.

§11.19 "Have you ever filed for bankruptcy?"

A lawsuit is an asset just like a TV, watch or house. A person filing for bankruptcy must disclose their claim or case in their filings, if the claim was known at the time the petition was filed, or if the claim arose while the bankruptcy proceeding was pending. Failure to disclose it is deemed a act of fraud and results in judicial estoppel. This means the current lawsuit would be dismissed.

If you represent plaintiffs, this is a question to ask during the intake process. If you represent defendants, this is something to check using PACER and to ask at deposition.

Plaintiffs who fail to list the lawsuit as an asset can sometimes amend their petition to add it, even if the case is closed and all the debts were discharged. The bankruptcy trustee can be asked to reopen the bankruptcy estate to administer the lawsuit. Some trustees will do that. Some will not. If a petition cannot be amended, the odds are high that the current litigation will be dismissed on grounds of estoppel or judicial fraud.

§11.20 "Have you ever sought Social Security benefits?"

This is something else often asked of deponents. If the witness' health or ability to work are issues in play, the content of an application for Social Security retirement or disability - even the fact of an application - can be a goldmine for lawyers.

An application for retirement benefits is a clear sign that the deponent decided to stop working on a part-time or full-time basis. That goes directly to the mitigation of damages.

As for disability benefits, and very generally, applicants for Social Security disability benefits (known by the acronyms SSDI and SSI) must generally attest in their application that they are unable to work in any capacity and should be granted federal disability benefits. Such representations, though, can limit or extinguish damages (e.g., lost wages) being sought by a plaintiff. If you represent plaintiffs, this is a must on your consultation checklist.

Note that in some situations, SSDI and SSI applicants do *not* have to claim an inability to work. The Social Security Administration automatically deems certain conditions as disabilities. These are known as "listed impairments." So it's important to know the basis for the application for disability benefits. If a person has a listed impairment, they are entitled to benefits whether they can work or not.

§11.21 "Did you take documents or materials from the workplace?"

Many people remove documents from the workplace when they intend to file a lawsuit. Sometimes these documents contain trade secrets, confidential customer information, or medical information. Removal of such material can expose them to serious civil and criminal liability.

It is important to ask clients during the intake process whether they taken documents, tangible items or electronically-stored information from the workplace. This includes physical documents, email forwards, photocopies or downloaded digital files. While the information can prove critical claims or defenses, the removal might place your clients in serious legal jeopardy.

§11.22 "Have you logged into computers or devices since your separation?"

It's not unusual for employees, contractors, vendors or others to access computer systems after their employment or business relationship ends. It's so easy to do, and so tempting to log in and grab whatever documents might seem useful. IT departments don't always block access as swiftly as they should.

But even if the person can still gain access, doing so is

likely a crime under any of the myriad of state and federal computer-crime laws. And there is always a perfect audit trail of such access – where, when, from what IP address, and using what login and password. The audit trail will also show what the unauthorized user accessed, and what documents were copied, forwarded or downloaded.

Again, this is an essential topic to discuss in every deposition prep session, if not long before.

And it applies equally to individuals and organizations. Sometimes defendants capture employee usernames and passwords when they access personal accounts on company systems. I have been involved in cases where, after a termination, the employer accessed the employee's personal email accounts to see what the employee was saying. The ease of access and perception that "no one will know" is sometimes too tempting to resist, but can lead to serious criminal charges.

§11.23 "What did you tell your [lawyer] [accountant] [spouse] [doctor] [pastor]?"

Clients are usually unaware of testimonial privileges. As a result, they may reveal highly-confidential information unless you counsel them early.

The topic of testimonial privileges is always on my deposition prep list, as well as on my new-client checklist. I explain the reason why privileges exist, and I offer examples of the many types: attorney-client, doctor-patient, clergy-parishioner, accountant-client, and the spousal privilege.

I've found that giving them an overview helps them understand what privileges are intended to do - allow people to speak freely and candidly where the subject is likely of great importance. I make plain that all communications with me, my lawyers, and my staff are all covered.

Finally, I explain how privileges are waived. If I am representing more than one person or entity, I stress that communications between them may not be covered by a privilege, even if they are talking about our pending legal matter. Great harm can result from a breach of the privilege and so time devoted to its parameters is time well spent.

§11.24 "Do you have his number on your phone? Do you have those documents in your car?"

Unbeknownst to you, your client might have all sorts of evidence in their pocket, on their phone, or in their car on the day of the deposition. Sometimes you might not even notice that they are carrying a folder or notebook into the deposition room, loaded with additional items they grabbed the day before.

It is important to talk about what to bring, and what not to bring, on the day of your client's deposition. Absent guidance, you might have some unpleasant surprises as the opposing lawyer randomly asks about something and your clients volunteer that they happen to have relevant documents in the bag at their feet. This touches again on the crucial important of managing every facet of the deposition.

§11.25 "Well, what would you have done if......"

Hypothetical questions can be a legitimate form of inquiry,

depending on the witness and depending on the question. Some courts hold they are improper if they seek to elicit opinion testimony from a non-expert, commonly citing FRE 602 (personal knowledge requirement), 701 (opinion testimony by lay witnesses), and 703 (opinion testimony by expert witnesses). There is no single rule, however, squarely addressing this issue. Courts sometimes disagree even as to what constitutes lay opinion testimony. Sec. & Exch. Comm'n v. Sabhlok, No. C-08-4238 EMC, 2010 WL 2944255, at *4 (N.D. Cal. July 23, 2010) (addressing dispute whether testimony from auditors was lay opinion or disguised undisclosed expert testimony).

But what clients can be asked in a deposition, and what can be used at trial, are two different matters. So if a hypothetical question is asked in a deposition, your client must generally answer it. You cannot properly instruct clients not to answer a hypothetical question solely on the ground it is hypothetical.

Rule 30(c) makes plain that all objections made at the time of the examination shall be noted and that evidence objected to shall be taken subject to objections. Absent a claim of privilege or of a harassing examination, instructions not to answer questions at a deposition are almost always improper. Shapiro v. Freeman, 38 F.R.D. 308, 311 (S.D.N.Y. 1965) ("It is not the prerogative of counsel, but of the court, to rule on objections. Indeed, if counsel were to rule on the propriety of questions, oral examinations would be quickly reduced to an exasperating cycle of answerless inquiries and court orders.").

Further, Rule 26(b) says "parties may obtain discovery regarding any matter, not privileged, which is relevant to the subject matter involved.... It is not ground for objection that the information sought will be inadmissible at the trial if the information sought appears reasonably calculated to lead to the discovery of admissible evidence."

It's best to alert your client to the possibility of hypothetical questions, and to include them in your mock cross-examination. Many hypothetical questions are incomplete and may require your client to engage in pure speculation. Unless your clients are cautioned about hypothetical questions - what would you have done, what would you do, what should have been done - they may buy right into it. They may even feel that answering a hypothetical shows the depth and breadth of their knowledge.

Often the proper answer to a hypothetical question is, "That isn't what happened, and I have no way of knowing what I would have done." You can use illustrations during deposition prep to show your client how an innocent hypothetical can lead them astray.

§11.26 "You have other documents? Would you give them to your lawyer, so she can give them to me?"

There are occasions where the opposing lawyer realizes during the deposition that your client has information or evidence the lawyer did not previously request. Once this happens, the next question is typically something like "Would you be willing to provide a copy of that your lawyers? So they can provide it to me?"

This request seeks to short-circuit the discovery process, which requires the opposing lawyer to serve a request for production and wait thirty days or more to receive the documents.

I ordinarily object or ask the lawyer to serve a proper request for production. Informal requests to deponents or their counsel (during depositions or during breaks) to produce documents are generally not enforceable discovery requests. So said one federal judge in a 2018 Memorandum Opinion. *Troutman v. Louisville Metro Department of Corrections et al.* No. 3:16-CV-742-DJH, 2018 WL 3873588, at *3 (W.D. Ky. Aug. 15, 2018.)

This kind of mid-deposition ask is so common that I am quoting verbatim the somewhat lengthy commentary by the court. The bottom line: If you need something from a deponent, follow ordinary discovery procedures using document requests, interrogatories or subpoenas.

From the judge's order:

"The common thread throughout Troutman's complained-of discovery requests is that they were all informally made. The informality of the requests serves as the primary basis for defendants' objections, with both defendants essentially stating that they tried to accommodate Troutman's requests as best they could. (DN 93, #644; 94-1, #652–53.) The informality of the requests is also the reason why Troutman's motion for sanctions based on them must be denied. Federal courts across the country have routinely denied motions to compel on the basis that the discovery requests were informally made. *See, e.g., Garrison v. Dutcher*, 2008 WL 938159, at *2 (W.D. Mich. April 7, 2008); *James v. Wash Depot Holdings, Inc.*, 240 F.R.D. 693, 695 (S.D. Fla. 2006). In *Sithon Maritime Co. v. Holiday Mansion*, 1998 WL 182785 (D. Kan. April 10, 1998), the District of Kansas explained why federal courts cannot grant motions to compel when the discovery requests are informal:

"The Federal Rules of Civil Procedure provide necessary boundaries and requirements for formal discovery. Parties must comply with such requirements in order to resort to the provisions of Fed. R. Civ. P. 37, governing motions to compel. Informal requests for production lie outside the boundaries of the discovery rules. Formal requests may be filed under some circumstances, not letter requests. Formal requests require certificates of conferring and service. Letters do not.

Formal requests certify representations of counsel under Fed. R. Civ. P. 11(b). Letters do not. To treat correspondence between counsel as formal requests for production under Rule 34 would create confusion and chaos in discovery." Id. at *2. See also *Studio & Partners, s.r.l. v. KI*, 2007 WL 896065, at *1 (E.D. Wisc. Mar. 22, 2007 (holding that an informal request for production for documents made at a deposition was not an appropriate discovery request under the federal rules) (citing

Roberts v. Americable Intern., Inc., 883 F.Supp. 499, 501 n. 2
(E.D. Cal. 1995)).

§11.27 "If you don't know, it's okay to say so."

Watch out. This is a trap laid by many lawyers, and it
preys on your client's natural desire to avoid conflict and to
get the deposition over with. Your clients do not appreciate
that saying "I don't know" in deposition likely precludes them
from offering a substantive answer at trial, or at minimum
allows the adversary to impeach the client's newfound knowledge with the prior deposition testimony.

"I don't know" often closes a door that can't be reopened.
With enough "I don't know's" in deposition, your client will
be unable to rebut what opposing witnesses will say in court.

§11.28 "I'm going to stand beside you and go through these documents with you."

I occasionally see lawyers get out of their chair, walk over
to my side of the table and stand next to my clients while they
review documents. Sometimes, lawyers will point to various
paragraphs in the document and inquire as they stand there.

I respectfully request that such lawyers return to their seat
and resume the examination there. I never want adversaries
standing over or next to my client during testimony. The risk
of intimidation, intentional or otherwise, is too high.

§11.29 "Have you now told me everything that is important about your claims?"

Beware this type of question if the examiner has only
superficially covered the claims or specific topics. It is rare,

unless the examiner is unusually thorough, that your client will have revealed absolutely everything of significance.

Further, your client may not know all the facts that are important to the legal issues.

Thus some of my clients have responded along the following lines:

I have fully answered your questions to the best of my ability and have not purposely withheld anything responsive to your questions. But if there are things you have not asked me about, then there may be things I have not told you. And I don't know what else the law says is important in this case.

It's essential to prep clients for this kind of question, because it's intended to make your clients look dishonest if they add anything more to their testimony at trial. It's an especially unfair tactic, too. Deponents only answer the questions asked. If the examiner does a poor job, the fault lies with the examiner, not with the deponent. The question ought to be turned back on the examiner: Have you now asked me about everything that is legally and factually important?

§11.30 "Have you and your partner ever separated? Have you ever been unfaithful in the relationship?"

On occasion, particularly in cases involving claims for emotional distress, there may be questions coming out of left field at your client. In one recent case – not mine - a defense lawyer asked the plaintiff whether her marriage had a history of infidelity.

The plaintiff's lawyer objected under FRE 412, which

addresses issues of sexual conduct. The defense lawyer responded that infidelity goes beyond mere sexual contact, which drew scoffs from the plaintiff's counsel. Eventually, dueling motions to compel and for a protective order were filed.

The problem, though, was that the plaintiff blurted out "Yes" before her counsel could instruct her not to respond.

Educate your clients about the possibility they may be asked surprise questions about deeply personal matters - about their sex life, divorces, relationships, marriages, children, mental disorders, criminal histories, chemical addictions - you name it. Tell them firmly they are not to answer those questions without a long pause, so that you may object and instruct them not to answer if needed.

Then be sure to drill your clients during your mock cross to see if they'll blurt answers out. Slip this kind of question in several places during the practice session. It will help get them ready if an adversary attempts to catch them off guard.

AFTERWORD

We hope you found this Five-Minute Guide useful. It's part of a series of short, expert-level guides authored by Jim Garrity, the nation's leading expert on deposition science and practice.

The Five-Minute Guides fill a critical gap for litigators. Many of you told us you wanted something thorough and current but also short and to the point. You also told us you wanted something you can easily slip into your bag and take with you to depositions.

We heard you. The Five-Minute Guide series is the result, and we are genuinely grateful to you for purchasing it. (Don't forget that you can also buy his complete 490-page practitioner's guide on expert-level deposition strategies and tactics on Amazon. Search for *10,000 Depositions Later: The Premier Litigation Guide for Superior Deposition Practice.*)

A few final thoughts.

Jim Garrity invites input. If you have tactics or strategies that you find effective in taking or defending depositions, Jim would love to hear about them, and possibly include them in the next revision of this book. You can communicate with him directly at Jim@JimGarrityLaw.com. (And if you have questions about specific deposition problems you're encountering, email him about those as well. He often responds directly, and may (with your prior express approval) post a generalized, non-identifiable response on the book's Facebook page to alert others to the problems and to his solutions.

Like and follow the Facebook page. Be sure to stop by the free companion Facebook page to this book. That's where Garrity regularly posts new tactics, strategies, and cases on depositions. Like and follow at www.Facebook/ TenThousandDepositionsBook to receive his posts in your news feed.

Let us add you to our limited mailing list. A few times each year, Jim Garrity sends updates about new strategies and cases to a free, subscription-email group of litigators who've signed up to receive them. These come out before they appear on the Facebook page or in the next edition of the book. We'd love to add you to the list. He sends no more than four per year, and, typically, it's half that because he respects your time. Please email Josh Siskind, Director of Marketing, at JoshSiskind@RossAndRubin.com with "Please add me to the private email group mailing list" in the subject line. That's it. It's completely free.

Ask for a seminar. Jim Garrity regularly conducts live, full-day deposition seminars around the country. These programs receive rave reviews because they allow for direct interaction between Jim and litigators interested in sharpening their deposition skills. They also feature discussions of his newest insights and of cases released since the publication of this book. Interested? Reach out to Josh Siskind, our marketing director, at JoshSiskind@RossAndRubin.com for details.

Thank you again.

Ross and Rubin Publishers, LLC

Made in the USA
Monee, IL
12 October 2023

44431536R10059